Disintegrating Pakistan-

Free Balochistan, Pashtunistan and Existential Crisis for Durand Line

Author:-

Vinay Joshi

Director- ICRR

(Institute for Conflict Research & Resolution)

Email:- icrr.delhi@gmail.com

Introduction:- Post Pulwama events convinced men in uniform from Rawalpindi that Indian political and military leadership have prepared their mind to take risk to put an end to Pakistan sponsored terrorism in India. With stunning air raid by Indian Air Force- IAF on Balakot camp in Khyber Pakhtunkhwa well within Pakistan has changed the dynamics of Indo-Pak conflict. It has imposed unbelievable cost on Pakistan by forcing it to deploy huge military force on LoC and IB. Also Pakistan air force spending sleepless night anticipating more surprise raids within Pakistan. In this booklet we will take a look at various warring ethno-linguistic nationalities in Pakistan and role of State of Pakistan in it.

On internal front Pakistan is facing ever growing unrest in Balochistan and Pashtun belt. Baloch freedom fighters are incessantly pounding Pakistani forces all across Balochistan inflicting heavy causalities. Pashtuns raising voice under PTM flag to end invisible regime of terror proxies in Waziristan.

Here we will take a look at current situation of India- Pakistan military stand-off post- Pulwama and the effects of heavy military deployment on Pakistan's economy, internal politics, ethnic insurgencies and Pakistan's relations with two Muslim neighbors Iran and Afghanistan.

Let's start with Balakot strikes.

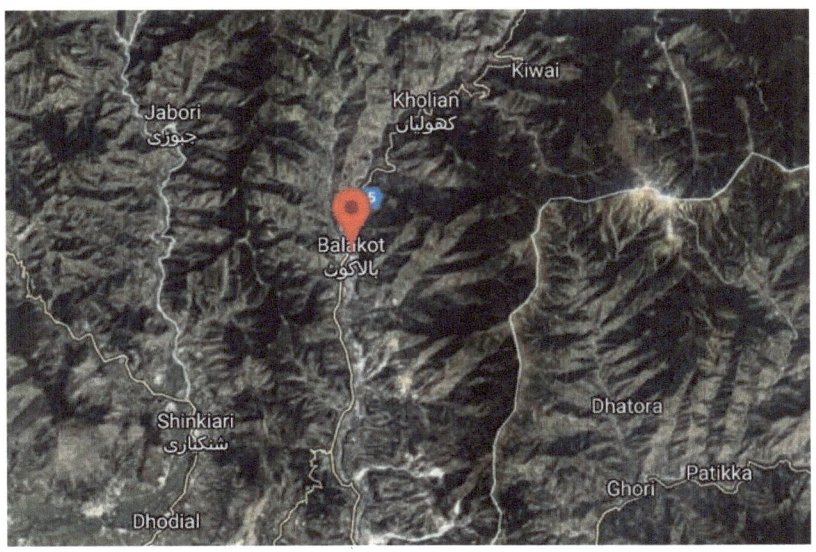

How to read Balakot Strikes?

India's surprise airstrike on Balakot Jaish e Mohammad- JeM camp well within Pakistan has drastically changed strategic equations in Asia. With air raids in Pakistan mainland, India junked its self-imposed strategic restraint policy against ISI sponsored terrorism. Earlier cross border commando raids by Indian Special Forces Units post- Uri had dealt severe psychological blow to Pakistan's proxies nurtured to bleed India. These SF raids were symbolic and sprawling terror factories within Pakistan largely remained intact. Anyone claiming PoK raids as perennial solution to Pakistan sponsored terrorism, were either cheating themselves or has no knowledge of terror ecosystem. But yes, these SF strikes sent shock waves in ISI and Pakistan's relentless nuclear intimidation discarded for once and all.

After post Uri cross border raids by Indian SFs, Pakistan's terror proxies changed their policy of getting entrenched for long in PoK fearing surprise Indian attacks. They used to change their locations to evade Indian surveillance. Not only that Pakistan's COAS General Bajwa visited LoC almost once or twice a month to close the gaps which could help Indian SFs to mount surprise attacks on terror launch pads. His visits were aimed at discouraging Indian forces from any sort of action crossing LoC and to boost the morale of his own troops.

Continuous Nuclear intimidation by Pakistan had created such a complacency and sense of security in Pakistani leadership, armed forces and terror proxies, that they never weighed on possibility of Indians using their air power to strike terror incubators within Pakistani mainland. Balakot has teared apart that complacency and reduced arrogance of ISI and Pakistan Army to rubbles. The mental shock was such a severe that, DGISPR himself declared that Indian fighter jets violated Pakistan airspace but dropped payload at empty jungle after getting scrambled by PAF jets. Actually it was mistake of DGISPR to accept IAF jets bombed Pakistani territory crossing PoK and without getting detected or encountered by their own jets.

Post Balakot- Where are JeM and JuD cadres now?

As per credible reports from Khyber Pakhtunkhwa and FATA, all anti India jihadi fighters have been relocated by ISI in Paksitan army garrison and forts in Pashtun belt of KPK and FATA. The area is hotbed of Pakistan's terror proxies like anti Afghanistan Taliban and anti Iran Jaish-Ul-Adl. The same area hosts unbelievable terror infrastructure created by ISI and CIA to mount Mujahiddin attacks against Soviet troops in Afghanistan. The area is homeland of Haqqani Network founder Jalaluddin Haqqani who was native of Miranshah town of same region. And Madrasa Haqqania founded by iconic Taliban founder Moualana Sami Ul Haq to which Imran Khans' PTI led KPK provincial government had given millions of dollars as government aid just few months ago.

Will Pashtuns stand shoulder to shoulder with Pakistan Army in case of War?

No! Scenario is totally different in Pashtun belt. Since 1948 first Indo- Pak war, Pashtuns were main force for Pakistan army in was against India. Taliban radicalization has further amalgamated Pashtuns with ISI and Army. But situation is rapidly changing since last one and half year. As per social media activist and various Kabul based analysts, extra judicial murder of young promising Pashtun singer and model Naqeebullah Mehsud by notorious trigger happy police officer Rao Anwar, Pashtun masses getting alienated from Pakistan.

Pashtun Tahafuz Movement democratic civil rights movement founded charismatic Manzoor Ahmad Pashteen has changed the narrative of Pakistan's Pashtun belt without any doubt. Before emergence of PTM and Pashteen; young creed of Pashtuns of Pakistan were zealously listening and singing songs of victory of Mujahiddins against foreign occupational forces in Afghanistan, but now every young Pashtun in Pakistan is going by PTM anthem "Da Sanga Azadi Da?" (What sort of freedom is this?) questioning atrocities committed by Pakistan Army against Pashtuns under the pretext of war against terrorism.

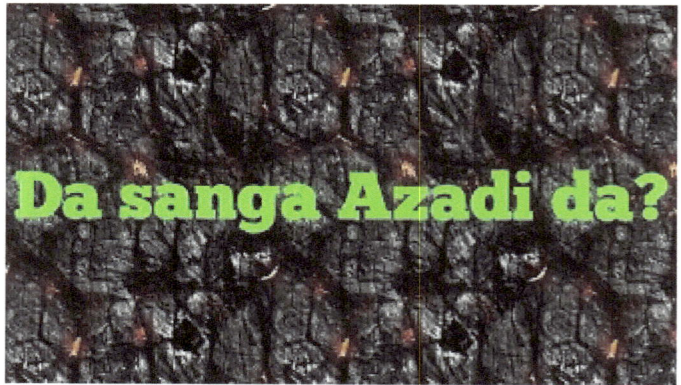

As per ground reports Pakistan Army had cordially invited tribal elders at Janikhel in North Waziristan to seek their support for war against India but, Malakand, Momand and Khyber elders flatly refused to be part of war efforts. Few months ago,

Member of National Assembly from Waziristan, Mr Ali Wazir had openly declared on social media, that don't count Pashtun support in any war; as war has only used Pashtuns as cannon fodder and Pashtuns won't repeat the mistake of fighting Pakistan Army's war!

No War is Actual War with Pakistan!

After Parliament attack in 2001, India had mobilized troops on Paksitan to pressurized it, but it withdrawn it after deploying them in eyeball to eyeball confrontation and after burning billions of dollars. After Pulwama, India mooted strong response and once again mobilized troops on Pakistan border. But current deployment is very different in nature. It has background of post Uri raids and Balakot strikes. There is biggest factor of unpredictability of decision making of Indian leadership. Pakistan is anticipating major infantry action by India to capture PoK. And warning India of using nuclear strikes. But nothing of that sort id going to happen.

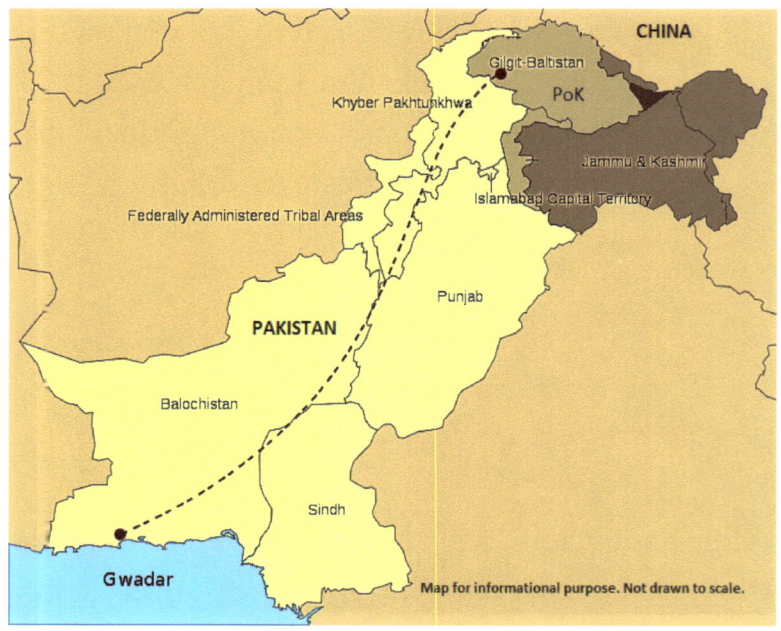

Map for informational purpose. Not drawn to scale.

Why?

As Pakistan economy is in shambles. It doesn't have money to pay their own government employees. US military aid has already stopped and Chinese infrastructure loan for CPEC piling at very fast pace. UAE and Saudi's bailout packages are of no use, as these loans won't salvage Pakistan's economy from ultimate collapse.

Heavy Indian military build-up on border will force Pakistan to maintain counter build up, which will further burn their precious dollars. Indian airstrikes have dealt severe blow to Pakistani civil and commercial air traffic. Pakistan's civil aviation has seen no activity since Balakot strikes. Even Chinese and many other international operators have stopped their airlines from flying in Pakistan air space. It has totally shook confidence of international players on Pakistan economy.

Moreover prolonged deployment of armed forces in combat posture will bleed the coffers and it will directly disturb domestic market shooting up inflation level. Such condition will directly affect internal politics and will trigger unrest against government and army if not handled properly.

War is Best for Pakistan, How?

If Pakistan with such a fragile economy enters war with India, it will open hundreds of opportunities for it to fetch dollars from world over. Pakistan will portray it as aggression of Hindu India on Islamic Republic of Pakistan. It will milch the war to tap deep pockets of radical Wahhabi and Salafi Arabs in the name of Islam. Also it will convince China to supply military hardware to teach India a lesson.

The Pashtuns, though very unhappy with Pakistan are fundamentally devout sunny Muslims. In case of full scale military hostility with India, many of them will stand by Pakistan Army severely hurting Pashtun cause. Pakistan will once again fool them in the name of Islam and the strong narrative developed by PTM, to seek equal rights for Pashtuns will take a dent.

So war without firing a single shot will be ultimate solution to bring Pakistan to its knees. Though it will cost India too, but much less than full scale military offensive and precious lives of Indian soldiers could be saved.

War of Attrition will pave the way for Independent Balochistan, Sindhudesh and Muhajir nation!

As soon as Indians mobilized troops along LoC and IB, Pakistan hurriedly started pulling its troops from Afghanistan and Iran border, only to redeploy them along Indian border. Pakistan's restive province Balochistan, which it illegally occupied in 1948 a year after independence; is heavily militarized province of Pakistan. Sensing military offensive from India, Pakistan vacated almost all military check posts from Balochistan, Khyber Pakhtunkhwa and FATA.

Baloch Liberation Army

The crazy withdrawal of troops emboldened Baloch freedom fighters, and so far almost 200 Pakistani military posts are overran, destroyed, looted or occupied by BLF, BLA, BRA or BA fighters. Hundreds of Pakistani troops, FC and Levies are killed in such encounters, which Pakistani media not showing up due to heavy censorship on its publication.

A senior Baloch commander expressed the possibility that consistent military pressure by Indian Army and aggressive deployment against Pakistan will break the backbone of Pakistani economy and bluff of military might of Pakistan will be destroyed. Such a aggressive posturing by India will give a golden opportunity to Baloch, Sindhi and Muhajirs to intensify their struggle against atrocious state of Pakistan. Baloch fighters and their unified command renamed and repacked under name of BRAS has already intensified their combat missions and their attacks against Pakistan forces have exponentially increased since February 15, 2019.

Israeli angle and Free Balochistan!

BALOCHISTAN

■ Pashtoon Area
■ Baloch Area

AREA   347,190 Km^2

6.511 Million

Number of Districts 27

------ Coastline ------

Immediately after Pulwama attack, Israel publicly declared support for India in war against terror. IAF fighters used Israeli smart bombs to pound JeM camp in Balakot. And chances are high that Israeli intelligence has provided cutting edge real time intelligence on Balakot to India. Israel's bitter rivalry with Iran has opened floodgates of opportunities for Independent Balochistan. To pin down Iran's global ambitions, Israel, USA and Saudi will need a good, secular, open minded friendly state in hand which must be in close geographical proximity with Iran. Free Balochistan fulfils all these criteria.

Baloch are historically secular, open minded and pluralistic society. They are intelligent and accommodating. Iran's Sistan- Balochistan province has huge Baloch population, where Baloch are being persecuted by Iranian Shia regime. Baloch Freedom groups always criticize Iran for atrocities on Baloch people in Sistan-Balochistan. Israel- Saudi- USA are in alliance to pin down regional and global ambitions of Iran. Pakistan, radically terrorist state is in cahoots with China, which is neither good option for anti Iranian schemes nor trustworthy partner for anti-Iran campaign. So best option for anti- Iran and anti- China global powers is Free Balochistan. Current Indian military build up against Pakistan will help achieving this goal.

Where China stands in Indo-Pak standoff?

China already dragged in Pakistan by its reckless $76 Billion investment in CPEC. Majority of these projects are unfeasible, delayed and marred with corruption. Also Baloch freedom fighters regularly targeting Chinese projects as they are accusing China of plundering Baloch resources without their consent and conniving with Punjabi Pakistan.

If Baloch leadership gives silent nod to Chinese investment and redraws terms and conditions of Chinese investment in Balochistan, then there is chance that China would remain moot spectator of Free Balochistan.

In any case it's not in Chinese interest to be party with either Pakistan or Balochistan when it has already invested so much in a shaky Pakistan. So, China will try its best to get assurance from emerging Baloch leadership (In case Balochistan going to be freed from Pakistani occupation) regarding its investment in Gwadar and other regions within Balochistan. Present armed Baloch freedom movement leaders including Dr Allah Nazar Baloch and Late Commander Ustad Aslam are in a no mood to spare Chinese assets lest they renegotiate with Baloch people for resources which China is exploiting from Balochistan.

Not only that late BLA chief Commander Ustad Aslam had sent his own son Rehan as suicide bomber to target Chinese bus on CPEC project and had released his video to motivate other

Baloch youth and to set example before people of Balochistan to fight Chinese economic subversion. Later Baloch fighters attacked Chinese consulate in Karachi to send strong message to Pakistan and China, Ustad Aslam released audacious video describing world community why they oppose Chinese investment and why they will continue to target Chinese investment in Balochistan.

Inference

Keeping in a view the complicated geopolitical situation in Indian subcontinent; China's growing ambitions to control Asia and Chinese need to secure its vital crude oil supply passing through Malacca Strait, China badly needs Balochistan. Pakistan is the name of temporary entity which broke up once in 1971 and about to break up in next few months.

So....

What India needs to do is.... Keep aggressive military build-up along LoC and IB to keep Pakistan Army on tows and to facilitate partition of Pakistan by supporting Baloch Freedom movement. If India refrains from major military conflict with Pakistan; it will deny Pakistan a chance to exploit the situation to mint money under the guise of Ghazwa-E-Hind from rich Wahhabi and Salafi elements.

Also Indian Military build-up on LoC without major military confrontation and frequent infantry/ air/ missile raids on Pakistani military posts and anti- India Jihadi elements deep within Pakistan will pave the way for immense economic pressure on Pakistan, which will ultimately break up Pakistan on ethnic lines vis. Baloch, Pashtuns, Sindhudesh and Muhajirs. The lasting solution for Kashmir issue and Afghanistan's Taliban menace lies in dismantling terror entity called Pakistan...

And....

This can be only achieved with doctrine of "No War Is Real War against Pakistan!"

Growing Pashtun Unrest Will end up erasing Durand Line?

Since 1947 Pashtuns devoted, sacrificed everything for the Pakistan. But in return they are payed back with atrocities, apartheid and bloodshed.

Pashtuns or Pakhtuns are second largest ethno-linguistic group of Pakistan. Though they are living in Pakistan since 1947, Pakistan's dominant Punjabi state apparatus never accepted them wholeheartedly as genuine Pakistani citizens. Any legitimate Pashtun grievance regarding government, Pakistan Army or institutions has always invited furious counter reaction from Punjabis and they are bluntly being labelled as 'Afghanis' for raising voice against state apparatus. Though Pashtuns are backbone of Pakistani Army, with representation more than their percent population, they bore the brunt of official state policy of creating, employing and mass killing by "Terror Proxies" viz. Taliban, TTP, JeM and LeT. The wounds are so deep and pains are so inconsolable that emotional schisms between Pakistani State and Pashtuns have gradually started widening. Now, they are on head on collision mode with the State of Pakistan to seek justice for whatever violence committed against them by state itself and state sponsored terror proxies. The whole Pakistan was inebriated with terrorist ideology but only Pashtuns were stamped with terrorism tag, shamed, blamed and killed for the crime which they never committed. Each and every time there is terror attack in Pakistan, LEAs used to hound, arrest and kill Pashtun youth by stamping them as TTP terrorist, only to hide real terror proxies.

Let's analyse the process.

How Pashtun unrest against Pakistan is valid?

Pakistan Army and intelligence agency ISI in collaboration with CIA converted predominantly Pashtun belt of FATA and Waziristan along "Durand Line" i.e. Afghanistan border as Mujahiddin's training, logistics hub and launching pads to mount bloody Jihad against Soviet troops in Afghanistan. Maulana Sami Ul Haq's Miranshah based Madrassa Haqqania was at center-stage of radicalizing Pakistani youth against Soviet occupational forces in Afghanistan. Radical Islamist youth from across the Pakistan flooded the Miranshah seminary to inculcate Jihadi ideology and to impart combat training to youth to fight against Soviet troops. Pakistani Punjabis and Muslim recruits from across the world in which Arabs were in large numbers flooded web of Madrassas founded, funded and operated by ISI's Jihad proxies. The combatants passing out from these seminaries defeated Soviet military with US logistical help and Pakistan's ISI's military training.

During the same period legendary Jihadi Jalaluddin Haqqani emerged as poster boy of ISI, who left tremendous footprint on Afghanistan Jihad. Haqqani was protégée of Maulana Sami ul Haq, but Haqqani achieved Islamic knowledge and combat skills at a time. Thus emerged Haqqani Network. It was war- drug trade- tax collection- smuggling network controlling many economic sources in Af-Pak region. Also it has hold over major chunk of military aid supplied by Americans to fight against Soviet. Thus Jalaluddin Haqqani developed unbelievable money and military muscle in very short span, which he employed to control drug trade and arms trade in the region.

Though all of these Jihadi activities were happening in Pakistan's Pashtun belt, traditional tribal Jirgas (Pashtun elder's councils) have no say in these issues. Anyone from these Pashtun Jirgas, who raised voice against misuse of their territory to wage war in Afghanistan had been brutally executed by ISI through Haqqanis. After Soviet withdrawal from Afghanistan, Osama Bin Laden emerged as key figure in Jihadi structure. ISI smartly created new proxy called Taliban which overthrown Afghan government and installed new regime which was directly controlled by Pakistan. Later Osama declared war on USA and ordered bombing of US embassies in Africa. Clinton bombed Osama's Afghanistan hideout but he had miraculous escape. After 9/11 attacks on US, coalition forces invaded Afghanistan and millions of Afghanistan refugees crossed Durand Line to enter Pakistan. Many Talibans also infiltrated refugees and took shelter in Pashtun areas to evade US raids. ISI received and cared them well. Pakistan redeployed them in FATA - Waziristan alongside Pakistani army camps.

Fake war on terror by Gen Musharraf- Primarily fought to milk US dollars!

Reeling under tremendous pressure of USA and mouth-watering American offers of military and cash aid, Gen Musharraf ordered Pakistan armed forces to enter FATA- Waziristan. Unbelievable military force was used against suspected terrorists, which were usually civilians. US agencies were merged with Pakistan army to oversee the Kill Rate on ground. The whole military offensive left precious Pashtun lives and villages perished and actual terror infrastructure intact.

Later in 2014, Pakistan army launched Operation Zarb-e-Azb, the biggest offensive in Pashtun belt, which left Waziristan totally destroyed. About million Pashtuns displaced and Pashtun homeland witnessed never seen before mass destruction. The so called War on Terror by Pakistani forces has left Pashtuns badly bruised and battered. More than 1.5 lakh Pashtuns perished during spurious War on Terror; moreover 65,000 houses and commercial establishments of Waziristan razed to the ground by indiscriminate, disproportionate and unethical air raids by Pakistani forces. Actually Gen Musharraf unleashed terror in Pashtun belt to earn dollars from USA by killing thousands of Pashtuns in an eyewash operation. Real terrorists were sheltered in Pakistan Army cantonments and helpless Pashtun civilians slaughtered in a broad day light. Even though Pakistan army continued to pat on own back as champion that defeated terror, Pashtuns slowly started rejecting its claim. The fallacies of victory of terror are aggressively being focused by Pashtun elders and activists.

Carefully planned segregation of Pashtuns in Pakistan's socio-political circles.

The Pashtuns which have seen destruction of Waziristan since 2001 to 2014's Zarb-e-Azb and also witnessed being labelled as terrorists for no valid reason have started rethinking their relations with State of Pakistan. They started demanding end of apartheid and equal rights. They repeatedly requested not to recklessly treat them as terrorist. They started raising voices against enforced disappearances and extrajudicial killings of Pashtun youths. And few incidences triggered democratic Pashtun uprising in Pakistan....

Naqeebullah Mehsud killing- Biggest game changer event in Pashtun politics.

A special tribute to Shaheed Naqeeb Ullah

شہید نقیب اللہ کا قصور کیا تھا

In January 2018 young Pashtun model, singer Naqeebullah Mehsud picked up by trigger happy police officer Rao Anwar. Police killed Naqeebullah in fake encounter terming him as terrorist. But his track record punctured police claims. The wave of anger swept Pashtuns and another young activist Manzoor Ahmad Pashteen called for democratic protest against killing of Naqeebullah. Thus Pashtun Tahaffuz Movement led the charge against apartheid. Within the first year of PTM, it has carved out great space for Pashtuns in Pakistan. It has stunned, confused and disturbed Pakistan's military establishment which is shadow ruler of the country. PTM's valid democratic position on all issues pertaining to

Pashtuns has left Pakistani army and ISI scrambling for cover. The confidence which PTM infused in Pashtuns resulted into common man blaming Pakistan army and ISI for the sins they committed since last many decades.

Kneejerk reaction to PTM by Pakistan Army and Intelligence agnecies.

Ever growing support to PTM and well organised public gatherings of PTM has left State machinery in a tizzy. In a hurried, haste response to clamp down PTM, state used rude techniques against PTM office bearers which proved counterproductive. First they arrested popular Pashtun activist Gulalai Islamail, then they released her after social media backlash. Then her name included in ECL list to prevent her from travelling abroad. In yet another move popular Pashtun Member of Parliament from Waziristan Mohsin Dawar and Ali Wazir placed in ECL and both were offloaded from Gulf bound flight. After much uproar state backtracked, but only after scoring big self-goal.

Abduction and killing of Pashtun officer SSP Tahir Dawar

In another shocking incidence senior Pashtun police officer of Peshawar police SSP Tahir Dawar abducted from high security Islamabad area and after two weeks his bullet ridden body found in Afghanistan. Furious Pashtun elders from Shinwari tribe residing on Torkham border entry point refused to hand over his body to interior minister Shehariyar Afridi. SSP's family refused to wrap Pakistan's flag on his body as state was behind his murder. Aggrieved crowd attending funeral chanted anti Army slogans in the very presence of political, military leaders including ministers. The anger against military and ISI was so high that many Pakistani social media users were shocked to see army and ISI being hurled with abuses in Pakistan.

The whole episode underlined eroding popularity of Pakistani Army and ISI. Also the same Pashtun youth which Pakistani establishment was taken for granted by them was taking about turn and refused to buy its jingoistic narrative. So far, establishment used to throw its sins under carpet by pumping aggressive religious sentiments and anti-India feelings among citizens of Pakistan. But the business of perpetual anti India hate mongering was over as non-Punjabi Pakistanis has started independent thinking on their own. For supporting Pakistan, Pashtuns got death and destruction in past 3 decades as a return gift, they are branded and defamed as terrorists for the Pan- Pakistani proxies created by ISI. Their liberal voices ruthlessly suppressed by Haqqani and Taliban proxies.

What would be the next? What would be the future of Durand Line? Is Pakistan heading towards Balkanization?

Beginning of the end of Durand Line?

PAKISTAN'S PASHTUN UNEASE THAT JUST TRIGGERED DURAND LINE COUNTDOWN

Durand Line which was drawn in 1893 by Britishers to divide Pashtuns, later became border between Afghanistan and Pakistan. But it has left 70% Pashtuns in Pakistan and just 30% in Afghanistan, even though they assume Afghanistan as land of Pashtun forefathers. Durand Line is most hated structure among Pashtuns and its existence pains them most. Till 1834 Peshawar was winter capital of Afghanistan, which is now in Pakistan. Afghanistan and Pashtuns are inseparable from each other. (https://twitter.com/AmrullahSaleh2/status/94126 5911436242944). Durand Line has separated it from Afghanistan and gifted it to Pakistan.

On March 16, 2019 Pakistani Parliamentarian from Waziristan, Mr Ali Wazir led the Wazir Jirga to cross Durand Line and to reunite forcibly separated Pashtun tribes by artificial. Pakistani agencies tried to resist them but they couldn't! Ali Wazir led Jirga members were warmly welcomed by Pashtuns from other side of Durand Line. The growing resentment among Pakistani Pashtuns will increase such solidarity gestures in near future.

Repeated requests by Pakistani Pashtuns to stop their humiliation in the name of actions against terrorism, their insulting profiling, enforced disappearances; extra judicial killings and violence against Pashtuns by State's Terror Proxies have fallen on deaf ears. People used to tolerate such humiliation by any country only when they don't have any good alternative. Pakistani Pashtuns have their ancestral land called Afghanistan just on the other side of Durand Line. Afghan Pashtuns which were living in Pakistan as refugee post 9/11 have reinvented their ethnic ties with Pakistani Pashtuns. They are treating them as their relatives. If Pakistan fails to read the writing on the wall, then Durand Line would be the biggest loser.

Whatever Ali Wazir- MP Pakistan Parliament did with Wazir Jirga, was not symbolic move. But it was manifestation of boiling anger against apartheid vis-a-vis Pashtuns; it was resolve to part away from Pakistan which misused beloved Pashtun land to breed terror proxies. It was beginning of the unification of Pashtun land mischievously partitioned by Britishers with Durand Line to rip apart Pashtun valour which defeated British Empire twice in a row.

For years together Pashtuns are rejecting Durand Line which divided ancestral Pashtun land between Afghanistan and Pakistan. Pakistan's abysmal track record as a democracy has added fuel in anti-Duran sentiments. Pashtuns sacrificed their valuable blood for the sake of Pakistan in selfless manner, but in return they only received stamp of terror on whole society. For every call for justice and equality in Pakistani society they were branded by stooges of GHQ as "traitors", "Afghanis", "terrorists". While abusing them, rulers and de facto rulers viz Pakistan Army and ISI conveniently forgot the truth, that whatever terror activity flourished in Pashtun land along Durand Line was manufactured by army and ISI. Thus blaming Pashtuns for the same is actually blaming policies of Pakistan.

What we can conclude- countdown of Durand Line has begun and it will meet the same fate like artificial Berlin Wall, which disintegrated in 1989. Will another fictitious and spurious entity will be thrown in the history on 30th anniversary of fall of The Berlin Wall? Probably yes!

Da Sanga Azadi Da – Emotional Cry of Pashtuns

Since its foundation a year ago, The Pashtun Tahaffuz Movement- PTM is asking painful question to Pakistan establishment- Da Sanga Azadi Da? –What kind of freedom is this? After series of big Jalsa- Public gatherings and sit in protests Pashtuns failed to get convincing answer to their valid question- Da Sanga Azadi Da? Within regular intervals extrajudicial killings, abductions and targeted killings of Pashtun activists are occurring. Latest custodial death of PTM central executive member from Peshawar Prof Arman Luni is most shocking of all. PTM has already declared huge gathering "Peshawar Long March 4 Arman" on March 31, 2019 to seek justice and to press for punishment to guilty officers. But neither PTM leadership nor Pashtun commoner expect any sort of justice from Pakistani rulers. They will continue to add insult to injury. They will continue to humiliate Pashtuns.

The struggle will go on until erasing ridiculous geographical entity called "The Durand Line". We are going to witness it in near future, as Churchill had once said, "Those who fail to learn from history are condemned to repeat it." Pakistan flatly refused to learn from 1971 Bengal debacle and it is going to pay for it in Balochistan and Pashtunistan very soon!

Even after 1971 humiliating partition of Pakistan; which was resulted due to linguistic- geographic apartheid and aggressive Punjabi- Pakistani nationalism shrinking space for Bengalis of East Pakistan, no one in present political and military set up is taking lessons. Relentless atrocities on Pashtuns and Baloch have dented their claims of Jinnah's Pakistan and dealt a decisive blow to concept of Islamic Republic of Pakistan. All non – Punjabi ethnic, geographic nationalities are desperately seeking their space in Pakistan. With every passing day non- Punjabi ethnic nationalities are getting convinced that separate nation is the only remedy for peaceful existence of their ethnicity. Situation getting changed with huge pace and Pakistan ultimately heading towards Balkanization!

Only time will tell- When?

www.ingramcontent.com/pod-product-compliance
Lightning Source LLC
Chambersburg PA
CBHW050757290526
45792CB000C8B/2224